# *OWNING AND OPERATING*

# *A SUCESSFUL*

# *CLEANING BUSINESS*

# *IN LESS THAN A WEEK*

# BE YOUR OWN BOSS
## OWN YOUR OWN BUSINESS
# START YOUR CLEANING SERVICE

Congratulations! You have made a wise choice. By purchasing this book, you have made the first step in owning your own business, getting out of debt and getting ahead in the financial game. In this book, I have eliminated all the trial and error and saved you from the trivial mistakes new business owners make. Owning your own successful business is only difficult if you don't know what to do and more importantly, how to get started. I've heard so many people say they would love to start their own business, but just don't know how or where to begin. Now you have the tools needed to get moving in the right direction. A cleaning and/or janitorial service can bring from $500 to $5,000 a month in your spare time – typically less than 10 hours a week. This type of business is something that can be done while keeping a nine to five day job. If you can contract with local real estate offices to clean their rental homes when a tenant moves out, it can be done after you get off from your day job or on the weekends. If you are cleaning an office, they will want you to come in after hours, while their employees are gone. If you are requested to come during the week, this allows you ample time – typically from the time they close (usually 5:00 p.m.) until they open the next day. If you are working on a weekend, then you have from 5:00 p.m. Friday evening until they open on Monday morning. It's the perfect second job to bring in that extra money needed to get ahead and get out of debt! No other part time job will pay you what you can make working for yourself. There is no overhead and supplies are minimal. You can do the work yourself without hiring employees and claim a home office on your taxes. The following pages are easy, simple, step by step instructions that anyone can understand. If you follow these instructions, you will own your own business in less than a week. All you have to do is get out there and make it happen. Here's wishing you a world of success!

CONTENTS:

TO DO LIST –

In four short steps, you will be the proud owner of your own business.

1. CHOOSE A NAME
2. DECIDE ON YOUR PHONE
3. APPLY FOR YOUR EIN (EMPLOYER IDENTIFICATION NUMBER)
4. OBTAIN YOUR STATE LICENSE

## CHOOSING A BUSINESS NAME

As much fun as it is to sit around with your friends and family thinking up a funny or catchy name, (anything that involves a play on words is always hilarious to me) but the truth is that people will remember something a little more simple and will instantly know what kind of work you do if you use the word "janitorial" or "cleaning" in your business name. Funny, cute names are just that – funny and cute. Make sure your customers take you seriously and reflect that in your business name. I prefer to use my last name in order to promote my business. Local people know me and therefore, recognize this as my company. Anytime you attend an event, whether it is business or social, make sure you introduce yourself to everyone you meet. If they remember you and your name, it could mean a new contract in the future if they come across your business name.

## YOUR BUSINESS PHONE NUMBER

The most efficient way to allow customers to contact you at any time is with a cell phone. Unless you want to be tied to a land line; i.e. stuck at home, this is your best choice. Also keep in mind, if a new potential customer calls and gets a recording on a land line when no one is home, nine times out of ten he will not leave a message or call back. It is a big turn off to call an office without reaching a live person. We live in an instant gratification society. People want information when they call, immediately. They do not want to wait for someone to call back. Also, think about what this says about your company. Your business must not be a priority to you if you do not answer the phone during normal working hours. If you have a day-time job and cannot answer the phone right away, you can at least call back on a break or during lunch. I use my personal cell phone and have changed my current contract to "free incoming calls". This way I can speak to any customer that calls me without being concerned about using too many minutes. If I need to make a call out and know that it is going to be lengthy, I use my land line at home and make a free call. Any cell phone company will have various plans to choose from. Do some research and find out which plan suits your particular situation best. You will need to make a decision on this before going any further. Your applications for EIN and bank accounts (as explained next) will ask for a business phone number.

EMPLOYER IDENTIFICATION NUMBER OR EIN

An EIN is an identification number used by the IRS to track your income and taxes, as well as identify your company on any forms you may fill out. You will also need this number to open a bank account in your business name and to apply for credit at any supply store. The contracts you win will need this number for their tax records as well. Some small business owners will use their social security number in place of an EIN. This is perfectly legal and would be fine if you only intend to have two or three small contracts at a time. However, I strongly discourage this practice and recommend obtaining an EIN. It is extremely important to keep your personal and business assets separate. When you are conducting business, you are acting on behalf of your business. When applying for credit, you will want to have your business income and assets considered, not your personal ones. Also, there is the issue of identity theft. Do you really want to read off your social over the phone to every potential customer, whether you have a signed contract with them or not? There are several websites out there that will charge a fee to obtain an EIN, but *do not* use them. Unfortunately these websites are a scam. Most will provide a legal EIN but will charge you for it. The official government website is free and will instantly assign a number to you – the others will charge a fee and may take up to two weeks or longer to mail it to you.

The website is –
http://www.irs.gov/businesses/small/article/0,,id=102767,00.html

(I recommend saving this website in your "favorites". It has a lot of good information and may be helpful to you in the future).

1. At the bottom of the page you will find a link that reads, "APPLY ONLINE NOW". Click here.

2. The next page will give you some important information about the purpose of an EIN, some of which I have already explained to you. At the

bottom of this page you will see, "BEGIN APPLICATION". Click this link.

3. You will see another page with various options. As an individual owning a business, you are considered a "Sole Proprietor". If you open your business with another individual, you will be considered a "General Partner". Both apply unless you decide to obtain an LLC. As a small business just starting out, you may not feel the need to protect yourself in this way. If you live in a small to medium size town and know your customers; some of them may be close friends and you would therefore, not anticipate much of a liability issue. However, as your business grows and you obtain more contracts, so does your chance of some unfortunate accident or mistake happening. Even though you will be protected with liability insurance, if a claim should exceed your coverage, you could actually lose personal assets (i.e., cars, boats, houses) if you become involved in a law suit. Therefore, the choice is yours. Please note that you can change your status with the IRS in the future if you decide at a later date to obtain an LLC. You will have to apply for a new EIN under this status, but as you will see, it is relatively simple. Once you have made this choice, click continue.

4. You will then fill in the blanks with basic information and be assigned your number.

Please print this page and save it in a safe place. Your official confirmation will come in the mail within a few weeks. Until then, you can use this number to obtain business licenses and open bank accounts, but you may not file any tax returns until this confirmation is registered within the IRS databanks and you receive your confirmation letter.

## BUSINESS LICENSE – STATE AND LOCAL

In order to begin soliciting for business, you must have a state license. Obtaining a state license will give you the legal right to solicit business in any city or township within that state. Once you obtain a cleaning contract within a specific city, you must then obtain that city's license *before you begin work.* It is extremely important that you do not let the city license slide for a few weeks or even a few days. If you are caught, the fines can be hefty, even upwards of $5,000. The point here is to make money, not loose it. Take the time to go to the city hall and make it legal. This is a risk that is just not worth taking. A state license can be obtained at your county court house and will typically run between $10 and $45 per year. A city license is bought at your city hall and will cost between $45 and $100 per year, depending on your local regulations. Please note these are estimates only. You will need to give these offices a call if you want to know the exact costs. Once you obtain these licenses, you are a legal business owner. Your local offices will send a renewal notice in the mail once a year, allowing you to mail your payment.

## BUSINESS BANK ACCOUNTS

Opening a checking account in the name of your business is important. This is the simplest way to keep track of your income and expenditures without "mixing things up" with your personal accounts. At the end of the year, when you are ready to pay taxes, this will make your records clear cut and avoid any mistakes. Most any bank you choose will have a small business account available. Some banks will even give you a discount if you have more than one account. I recommend choosing one that a) has a very low or no monthly charge and b) offers online banking. This account should be used more or less as a deposit account. It would typically have very little activity each month, such as deposits from your customers, an occasional withdrawal for supplies and owner withdrawals. Online banking is a must for me. I can pull up my account at any given time and see the latest transactions, making sure that I haven't forgotten any transactions by matching my balance with theirs. I can transfer money into my personal account at any time. And I can see how much money I have made – definitely a motivator to keep growing your business!

FORMS - SAMPLE MARKETING LETTER, BUSINESS CARDS AND CONTRACTS/BIDS

### MARKETING LETTERS

Aside from the obvious, such as joining the local Chamber of Commerce and asking friends and family, there are a lot of good ways to obtain new contracts. Of course, you can advertise in the local paper or telephone book. Putting up flyers can sometimes bring in new business. I have also looked up local businesses that would be good prospects in the phone book. Another suggestion is to take a drive around town or in an industrial area. Remember the bigger the building, the more you can charge to clean it. However you get the information, at times you will hear of an office that is unhappy with their cleaning service or you may have a friend in an office whose current cleaning crew's contract is up. This is an excellent time to do some marketing and try to win that contract.

I have a marketing form letter I use for these occasions that allows me to plug in the business contact name and address. Call the main number and ask for the name of their office manager or "someone who handles your cleaning services". Use that name along with their address to send the marketing letter. Then make a phone call to each office within 3 to 4 days after mailing these letters. The conversation goes something like this: I sent you a letter a few days ago regarding your janitorial service. Do you currently have someone who cleans your office? If the answer is no, ask if you can come by to take a look at the office and put in a bid. If they respond that they do, in fact, have a cleaning service, say something like this: Are you happy with their services? This always catches people a little off guard, but really gets them thinking about whether they might want to try someone new. Offer to give them a trial period, say a few weeks or one month. Tell them you would be more than happy to prove your company does great work and that all services are guaranteed. If the office manager says no, he is happy with his current service and thanks you for calling, be sure to say thank you for his time, be courteous and ask that he keep you in mind if circumstances change in the future. You would be surprised how many office managers will remember you as the person who was very courteous and would probably be easy to work with. You will be the first company called a few months down the line when a new cleaning service is needed.

Another good idea is to always give your cell phone number to the office manager. Tell them they can call you day or night if any problems or special requests arise and you can have it taken care of immediately. This extra customer service strategy has won several contracts for my business. The funny thing is, not one office manager has ever called me after hours to request anything! They just like the security in knowing that option is available. On the following page, you will find a sample marketing letter. Please feel free to change this as suits your needs, or write your own if you wish. Giving this letter your personal touch will make it your own.

# MARKETING LETTER

***DATE***          (insert logo and contact info.)

Mr. Doug Smith
Dynac Corp.
2180 Fifth Avenue
New York, NY 11779-6909

Dear Mr. Smith,

We at Fred's Cleaning Service know how important it is to have a clean, comfortable facility - and how difficult it is to find a cleaning service that guarantees your satisfaction. You need a cleaning service that views its job in cleaning your facility as priority number one - delivering dependable, professional service at all times.

Fred's Cleaning Service understands the important day to day tasks of office managers. We have created a program that addresses all of your cleaning needs, including supplying your trash bags and bathroom paper products. Our goal is to eliminate your need to spend time on cleaning and supply issues, allowing more time for more important business matters.

Please contact us at the above number if your would like a bid on your office cleaning or if you have any questions.

Sincerely,


*** Your name ***
President

## BUSINESS CARDS

Having business cards printed professionally at a local print shop is extremely costly and highly unnecessary. I rarely see the actual card in anyone's roldex, it is usually written on a note card or found on a slip of paper on a bulletin board. However, it is very convenient to have them ready and available in case you happen to run into someone while out running errands or at a social function that starts asking questions about your business. (Always be on the lookout for new business!) I printed my own using a software called Print Shop, the cost ranges from $30.00 to $150.00, depending on which version you choose. There are some excellent graphics to choose from and you can play with the text until you get it just right. Make sure you include your business name, your name and your business phone number. I have also included a small line of text at the bottom that reads "Licensed, Bonded and Insured". This small line of text will let your potential customers know that you are a serious business owner that they can depend on.

Once you have your masterpiece saved, printing them out is so much more convenient than re-ordering from a professional printing company, waiting a few days or a week and then driving to pick them up. The quality will depend on what type card stock you buy for printing, but as I said, it is not necessary to spend a fortune on something that will more than likely be thrown away.

## CONTRACTS/BIDS

In the next few pages, you will find a sample contract/proposed bid that covers the basics, i.e. every cleaning aspect in a nutshell and how much you will be paid. Once I have determined the pay I would like to receive, I print this out as a proposed bid, signing my name at the bottom as an agent of my company. The office manager will either accept this bid, sign and return to me or come back with a counter offer. This will be explained in detail in the next section. This sample contract is intended as an agreement between two companies that eliminates any misunderstandings. Please keep in mind that this agreement is a binding contract. If you forget or are not willing to perform any job that you have agreed to, you have broken the agreement and that company can legally discontinue your services. On the flip side, this contract also assures that you are owed the amount agreed upon. Please note that is only a guideline and each individual office will have their own requests. Some office managers will want you to come in once a week and others may want two or three times a week. Normally this depends on how many employees they have and whether or not they have significant traffic from their customers. I have one contract that sees customers only in the lobby. Therefore, I clean the lobby and foyer areas twice a week to keep it looking clean and inviting. The following is a sample contract to get you started. You are welcome to copy and change this as suits your needs.

**SAMPLE CONTRACT**

**DATE**

PROPOSED BID FOR:

Mr. Gary Farmer
J & J Electric
4250 Azalea Drive
Birmingham, AL 36360

# SERVICES TO BE RENDERED ONCE EACH WEEKEND:

*All trash will be emptied and removed
*All restrooms will be cleaned and sanitized; supplies will be replenished
*All office furniture and horizontal surfaces will be cleaned and/or dusted
*All tile floors will be swept and moped
*All carpet will be vacuumed
*All front door facings and/or glass will be cleaned
*Coffeepot and any dishes in sinks will be cleaned
*Microwaves and refrigerators will be cleaned inside and out

# SERVICES TO BE RENDERED EACH TUESDAY AND THURSDAY:

*All trash will be emptied and removed
*Public restrooms will be cleaned and sanitized; tile floors will be swept and moped
*Foyer carpet floor will be vacuumed
*Entrance tile floors will be swept and moped
*Front door glass will be cleaned
*Engineering Department, hallway, Dispatch Service Area and kitchen tile floors will be swept and moped
*Engineering restroom will be cleaned and sanitized; floor will be swept and moped

## TO BE CLEANED THOROUGHLY ON FIRST VISIT, THEN ON AN AS NEEDED BASIS:

*Baseboards
*Light Fixtures
*Artificial Plants
*Windows

## SAFETY AND BOARD MEETINGS:

Break room and Conference room will be cleaned immediately after any safety meeting or before any board meeting, upon request, without additional charge.  Cleaning will include trash removal, wiping down all surfaces, vacuuming carpet and washing any dirty dishes.

## SUPPLIES:

All cleaning supplies and appliances such as chemicals, mops and vacuums are furnished by Fred's Cleaning Service.  Fred's Cleaning Service will provide trash bags, as well as kitchen and bathroom paper products at cost plus 10%.

All services are <u>guaranteed</u>.  We do not anticipate any problems; however, if you should have a concern or require a special service, we will have it completed to your satisfaction <u>before the following business day</u>.

PROPOSED BID:.........................................................$X,XXX per month

J & J ELECTRIC AGREES TO PAY FRED'S CLEANING SERVICE $X,XXX ON THE 10TH DAY OF EACH MONTH FOR THE PREVIOUS MONTH'S SERVICE, AS LISTED ABOVE.  THIS CONTRACT WILL BEGIN JULY 1, 20??, AND WILL TERMINATE ON JUNE 30, 20??.


_____          _____
J & J ELECTRIC                          FRED'S CLEANING SERVICE

# BIDDING ON AND WINNING NEW CONTRACTS

When visiting an office to obtain information for a bid, ask the office manager to show you around. You will need to see every square foot in order to obtain an idea of what you will bid. Several factors will determine what you propose as a bid. Ask questions and write everything down so that you can review it later.

1. How often will you clean? Once a week, twice a week or just the garbage on Wednesdays? Ask the office manager what he wants. He will normally have a standard that has been done in the past and will want to continue with it.

2. What is the square footage? This will help you determine how long it will take to complete your job.

3. Will you provide all cleaning supplies, such as Comet, Windex, etc.? What about garbage bags and/or paper towels and toilet paper?

4. How many bathrooms? They take a little more time than an office.

5. How many rooms are tiled versus carpeted? Moping is more time consuming than vacuuming.

6. How large is the kitchen and will you clean out refrigerators and microwaves?

7. Is this a public office with a lot of customer traffic?

Remember most office managers are hiring you to keep their offices clean in order to 1) impress their customers and 2) keep employees happy. If the manager only wants you to work once a week, ask if the offices stay fairly clean from one week to the next. Does the garbage pile up a little too much? These questions may prompt him to change from once a week to a twice a week schedule. If he hesitates, remember to confirm that you would be willing to do this on a trial basis, if he so chooses. It can be written into a temporary contract that lasts a few weeks or one to two months. That way there is no commitment and you have a better shot at getting your foot in the door.

Begin determining your bid proposal by finding out how long it will take. Let's say you have a building with the square footage of 10,000. This will take an estimated 2 to 3 hours with two people working, depending on how much tile to be moped and how many desks to be cleaned. (This is absolutely possible - you will be surprised at how efficient you become over time.) Make sure you pay yourself what you are worth. This all depends on what size city you live in and the cost of living index there. I personally wouldn't work for less than $25 per hour. Keep in mind you will pay taxes on this income and will have to buy supplies periodically. Therefore, $25 per hour times 2 people times 3 hours per week equals $150.00 per week or $600 per month.

$25 times 2 people = $50
$50 times 3 hours = $150
$150 times 4 weeks = $600

Sounds like a great formula to use, but what about that extra weekend every three months? If you don't compensate yourself for this, you will be working for free once every quarter. Use the following formula to determine an average over the year.

$150 times 52 weeks in the year = $7,800
$7,800 divided by 12 months = $650

In this case, you have compensated for that extra weekend by another $50. Of course, if you feel the work will take more time, or you live in an area that pays more, bump up the numbers as you wish. The worse thing that can happen is you will get turned down and the office manager will come back with a counter offer.

If you are bidding on a cleaning service for a house, the process is very similar. You must determine how many hours it will take and bid accordingly. Cleaning a house requires jobs like oven cleaning, scrubbing the tile showers, cleaning all windows, etc. Houses typically take longer because the kitchens and bathrooms are more time consuming. For example a 2,000 square foot home will take anywhere from 3 to 5 hours. In this case, I would charge between $75 and $125. The following is a list to get you started. It will give you an idea of what a realtor might expect from you.

# CLEANING LIST - HOUSES AND APARTMENTS

## KITCHEN
CLEAN REFRIGERATOR, INSIDE AND OUT, INCLUDING FREEZER

WIPE OFF COUNTERTOPS

CLEAN OVEN OR WIPE OUT OVEN

WIPE OFF STOVE TOP

REPLACE DRIP PANS OR SCRUB OFF DRIP PANS

WIPE CABINETS AND PANTRY, INSIDE AND OUT

## BATHROOM
SCRUB OUT TOILET AND TUB WITH COMET

WASH ALL SURFACES WITH CLOROX CLEANER

WIPE CABINETS, INSIDE AND OUT

CLEAN MIRRORS

## MISCELLANEOUS
REMOVE ALL GARBAGE

VACUUM ALL CARPETS

SWEEP OUTSIDE ENTRANCES, FRONT AND BACK DOORS

CLEAN ALL LIGHT FIXTURES

SPOT CLEAN STAINS ON WALLS, DOOR FRAMES AND LIGHT SWITCHES

CLEAN ALL WINDOWS, INSIDE AND OUT

SWEEP AND MOP TILE FLOORS

CLEAN BASEBOARDS

Cleaning a house will take anywhere from three to five hours, depending on the square footage and how much you need to do. Some tenants will have the house basically in good shape. Others will not even bother to take out the garbage. Always charge accordingly. Remember that realtors will want the house to look good for the next potential rental customer. This means paying a little extra attention to details like windows, baseboards and light fixtures. At the end of this book, I'll give you some great tips to accomplish this more quickly and efficiently.

The greatest thing about owning your own business is that you don't have to accept the job if it doesn't pay enough. You be the judge and don't sell yourself short. One trick I have learned is to ask what they would like to pay or what was paid in the past. Always bump this number up a few notches. Explain that your company will provide quality dependable work each week and this peace of mind will be well worth the extra dollars spent. Play on the fact that the reason you are there giving a bid right now is because they were unhappy with their previous cleaning service and quality is worth the money. Remember the old saying, "You get what you pay for".

PROVIDING A GUARANTEE

The most important part of owning a business is keeping your promises. If you say you will clean an office on a weekend that happens to fall on a holiday, guess what? You still have to clean it. What happens if you are sick? I've gone to work with a fever of 102, and it didn't kill me. I wasn't the most pleasant person to work with, but I kept my contract and got paid. It wasn't easy but I reminded myself that I was working for my own company and not punching a clock and working my tail off to get someone else rich! Keep your goals in clear view and provide the work you promised – it goes a long way and will get your customers to give you referrals to other businesses as well. The guarantee that I have always provided goes like this –

> "All services are <u>guaranteed</u>. We do not anticipate any problems; however, if you should have a concern or require a special service, we will have it completed to your satisfaction <u>before the following business day</u>."

> A translation in layman's terms – "If I forget to mop the kitchen floor, you are welcome to call me out on it. I'll be in that evening to correct my mistake."

Office managers appreciate this option and want to know that they can contact you with any problems. In fact, tell them you *want* them to be happy with your work – it makes a big impact and will win them over every time.

LIABILITY INSURANCE AND BONDING

Liability insurance protects you against property damage (for example: you accidently break an expensive piece of equipment or furniture or even a window) and bodily injury (for example: someone slips on your wet floor that was just mopped and breaks a bone). Most office managers will require this coverage with at least a $100,000 limit, a select few will not even ask. The cost is usually a few hundred dollars a year and can be paid in installments. I would absolutely obtain this insurance before starting work – even before you receive the keys to the building. If you don't have the funding before you start, wait until you get that first check and then go obtain your insurance. I wouldn't take a chance that some unfortunate accident could, in effect, close my business for good. However, I will say that I have never had the unfortunate circumstance occur that I had to use my liability insurance - I just don't believe in taking chances.

There are several different types of bonds available, such as surety and fidelity. What you will purchase with this business would be a fidelity bond. This will cover you in the event that your employee steals from the office you are cleaning. If you are working with a family member, such as a husband and wife cleaning team, you obviously do not need this coverage. However, many people do not fully understand what a bond covers and will consequently ask you to have one. I have a $10,000 bond with a premium of $100 per year. It is relatively inexpensive and worth the price if it means winning a contract that pays $8,000 to $10,000 a year.

Any insurance company can provide liability and bonding insurance. However, an independent agent has the option of getting quotes from several different insurance companies and therefore, can provide you with the best coverage at the lowest cost. Look in your yellow pages under insurance agents and find *independent* agents – they will give the best price and usually, the best personal customer service.

SUPPLIES: WHAT YOU'LL NEED & THE BEST PLACE TO GET IT

The best thing about owning a janitorial service is the minimal start up costs. I've learned over time what works, what doesn't and what costs less. The following is a list of supplies you will need.  The majority of these items you probably already own and can use to start your new business.

1. Windex – I just like this brand, the cheaper ones don't work well at all and the industrial strength brands smell like strong chemicals.

2. Comet – tried and true old favorite, but Ajax works well also.

3. Clorox Cleanup – Nothing kills germs like Clorox.  I use this on the bathroom sinks and toilets to insure they are sanitized, I have a spray bottle of Clorox cleanup and a large gallon size to refill as needed.  Please note: This is a great product, but never use it on granite countertops or they will be ruined!  Be careful to never spill on carpets.  Bleach stains are permanent!

4. Toilet Brush with accompanying holder – cheap ones work well, no need to go overboard on this one, just make sure it will reach under the rim – Teflon ones work great.

5. Duster – I like the "Original California Duster" from any car parts store, it costs about $3 and will pick up dust better than anything else I've tried.  Plus, it is washable and re-useable.

6. Broom – once again, any broom you choose will do the job; you can even use your household broom to save the cost of a new one if you wish.

7. Dust Mop – this one is optional; I have found it to be much easier to sweep a large area with these.  However, if you are sweeping small areas only, leave this supply out until you absolutely need it.  They are available at any hardware or home improvement store for around $20.

8. Dust Pan – the kind with a handle eliminates bending over and will really save your back – can be purchased at a hardware or home improvement store for around $10.

9. Disposable Gloves – Latex gloves similar to those used in hospitals and doctors offices work best.  If you have a latex allergy, silicone ones are available.  They can be purchased at any dollar store but are much cheaper at a janitorial supply.  I buy mine by the case and save quite a bit.  You will absolutely need these when cleaning bathrooms and kitchens.

10. Mop – Industrial size with removable head, so that it can be washed and dried periodically. Once again, available at any hardware or home improvement store. I prefer the mop heads made of more durable rayon. Cotton ones do not hold up as well with washing and drying – they have a tendency to fall apart.

11. Mop Bucket, Industrial size – bought at a hardware or home improvement store, make sure you purchase one with wheels. Imagine carrying 4 or 5 gallons of water through an office – not only back-breaking but the possibility of spills could be disastrous.

12. Paper towels – any cheap version will do, these will be used on windows only, therefore buying expensive brands is not needed

13. Rags – I have purchased large packages of cheap wash cloths at department stores for under $5. I prefer white ones due to the fact that I wash and bleach them after each use. If you have a few old ones around the house that have seen better days, you could certainly use these and forego the expense of new ones.

14. Basket – Buy a small basket, preferably with a handle, to keep all of your supplies in, available at any department or dollar store. You will be able to carry everything with you as you go from room to room, saving time and energy. You certainly do not want to be running back and forth looking for what you need.

15. Pine-Sol. This is what I use for general mopping. I prefer the orange scent and my customers always comment on how fresh and clean their offices smell. This works well on regular vinyl tile in kitchens and bathrooms. I have even used it on old wooden floors, but be very careful. Nice, new wood floors need special care – NEVER use water and Pine-Sol on an expensive wood floor.

16. Vacuum – Any vacuum will do. You can even use your household vacuum for now if you would rather not purchase a new one. Of course, you may have the inconvenience of carrying it back and forth to the job site, but once the money starts coming in you will be able to purchase an inexpensive one to keep at work. I have used both upright and canister vacuums as well as bag vacuums and bagless. It's definitely a plus to have a bagless vacuum for obvious reasons (no bags to buy!) but I can't

tell a significant difference in the way they work. Both have served me well so go with what works best for you.

If you should acquire a new contract that has any fixtures, floors or new materials you have not worked with before, I suggest you look up cleaning and care online. I've learned a lot about wood flooring, granite countertops and ceramic tile from several different websites. Another good source is a janitorial supply company. They can tell you what works best and, more importantly, what will work safely. Just keep in mind that "trial and error" is not an option when working on someone else's office. You wouldn't want *your* expensive new hardwood floor ruined and the office manager won't be happy about it either.

HIRING EMPLOYEES, THE PROS & CONS

Hiring employees is probably something you will want to do eventually. Even though office cleaning can be very simple and quick, it is still physical work and can be tiring – especially if you have a large area to be moped. Another good reason to hire employees is you will more than likely make enough money to go on a nice (well deserved!) vacation and will want to know your business is in good hands while you are gone. However, having an employee means keeping up with payroll, taxes and government filing. It can be a nightmare if you don't know the steps (watch for my next book - coming soon!). What works best in this situation is having a relative or close friend informed about your specific steps in cleaning and the days you clean. A week or two before you intend to take time off, have them come with you and observe what you do. Write a step by step plan for them to follow and check off as they go – that way you insure nothing gets left out. The last two times you clean before you leave for vacation, have them do the entire job *by themselves*. Don't lift a finger to help. Do nothing but answer questions and have them write down your answers. That way they have an absolute understanding of what will be expected of them and you can leave for vacation with peace of mind. I would also suggest you do this in case of emergency. Many people have a husband and wife team or even two close friends. But what happens when one of you becomes severely ill or has some other emergency and cannot possibly be there? Always have a back up! If you have a friend or relative that could use some extra money from time to time, this is your perfect back up person. Keep them informed of the process, as outlined above, and you will always feel free to take an occasional weekend off. Just make sure to pick someone and get them trained right away. If you have a contract with an office and you default on that contract, they have every legal right to cancel. Don't let your hard work go down the drain. Keep this safety net in place just in case of emergencies and you will always have this extra income.

TAXES

Paying your taxes will be a lot simpler than you think – and can make a world of difference in your deductions.  You absolutely must report every penny of your income to the IRS, there is no way around this.  Each contract you have that pays $600 or more for the entire year will file a 1099 – Miscellaneous Income report with the IRS and will mail you a copy.  This will include the total amount of money they have paid your company for the year.  You must file this with your state and federal taxes and you will be required to pay taxes on this income.  However, the deductions you can take will offset your taxes tremendously.  I have a filing system that works wonders for me.  Make a file for each month of the year to keep your receipts in.  These receipts will include every single purchase you make for your business, such as toilet paper, paper towels, Windex, Comet, etc.  However, here's the great part of owning your own *home-based* business.  You are allowed to deduct part of your mortgage, your utility bills, and your phone bills, even the mileage on your vehicle used for business.  Some home improvements will be tax-deductible.  Office furniture, office equipment, paper, pens and paper clips are all deductible.  Every time you make a purchase, ask yourself if this could be business related.  Even if you only spent a few dollars, keep those receipts!  It only takes a second to toss that receipt into a file and you will be amazed at how they add up.  Your accountant will appreciate the organized way you have kept up with everything and you may get some tips from them on other deductions unique to your situation.  If you are good with numbers and do your own taxes, Turbo Tax is great software that I use every year and highly recommend.  This software walks you through step by step and I feel very confident that I get every penny back in taxes that I should.

I must give a word of caution though, if you find after your first year of business that you are paying more in taxes than you anticipated, there are some precautionary steps you can make.  One way to offset this amount is to make a change in your W-2's in your regular day job.  Your employer can take an extra deduction out of your paycheck to offset the taxes you pay in your business.  Sometimes even $40 each pay period can really help.  Another way to make sure you have that extra cash at tax time is to save it.  Keep a specific amount of your business income in an interest bearing bank account.  Make that deposit every month and don't touch it.  Any amount you save, whether it is 10% to 25%, will help pay your taxes.  Another way to offset the owed tax amount at the end of the year is to make quarterly payments to the IRS.  This can be done online and is relatively simple.  Once you enroll, you can make weekly, monthly or quarterly payments – even set up a recurring schedule to have your bank account automatically drafted in the amount you choose. The following describes in detail the enrollment process.

ENROLLING IN EFTPS – ELECTRONIC FEDERAL TAX PAYMENT SYSTEM

Go to https://www.eftps.gov/ - save in your favorites – and click on enrollment. There you will see the following:

> Basic Enrollment Information
>
> I would like to enroll as:        A Business
> An Individual

Click on "Individual"

Scroll to the bottom and click on "next"

After reading the Privacy Act and Paperwork Reduction Act, click on "Accept"

The next page will ask for basic information; i.e. name, social security number, address and phone number. Fill these out and click on "Next"

The next page will show the address you entered and the closest U.S. Postal Service match. (Normally, these are the same) Click on "Select This Address" on the Postal Service match.

This may take you back to your contact information page if the address changes slightly. If so, just click "next".

The next page will ask for your financial institution information. You will need your bank routing number, account number and whether it is a savings or checking account. (Remember if you are paying as an individual, you would need to use your personal account. It is never a good idea to pay personal taxes out of your business account.) Then click "next"

At this point, you can set a limit on how much money can be drafted from your account. This is a good idea if you are concerned that someone may "hack" into your account. Whatever limit you choose, enter it here and click "next".

This is the confirmation page. Check to make sure all information you have entered is correct. If you need to make changes, click on the "previous" button and do so now. Then click "next"

The next page describes the debit authorization agreement and the disclosure authorization agreement. You must type in your name and social security number again. This will suffice as your electronic signature. Click on "accept"

The next page contains your enrollment trace number and the following information:

Here are the next steps now that your EFTPS Enrollment is completed:

1.  Your enrollment information will be processed immediately.

2.  Within 15 business days, you will receive further information by mail, including:

    •   your Personal Identification Number (PIN).

    •   a Confirmation/Update Form containing all your enrollment information, with updating instructions if needed.

    •   instructions on how to obtain your Internet Password.

If you do not receive your PIN and Confirmation /Update form within 15 business days, please call Customer Service at 1-800-555-8778.

Print this page for your records. I've included the customer service number here, for future reference in case you do not receive your PIN or confirmation form.

## CLEANING – TIPS TO MAKE IT SIMPLE & EASY

Now that we've gotten through the paperwork, forms and tax questions, it's time to discuss the actual job you will be performing. Believe it or not, this is the easiest part of all! Once you get into a routine and learn the steps to make it simple and efficient, you will find that it's really not that hard and takes much less brain power than probably any other job you have had. The following are step by step instructions for each type of room you may be cleaning. I have included this on a separate page so that you may print it out or copy it and take it with you on the job. With some extra space for notes, you can make a copy for each office you clean. Write in your notes and any special needs for that office. Make sure you have a copy of these for your backup person. These simple rules will also apply if you clean houses, except you can eliminate the offices. In fact, cleaning houses can be done even more quickly and efficiently in rental homes, since there is no furniture.

Once you have a system in place for each office, you will get faster and more efficient. If you do everything needed in each room before moving on, it will take considerably less time than you would imagine. What I like to do is keep everything on a cart (if the office you are cleaning provides one) or in a basket so that I am not walking back and forth to get what I need. Bring along all of your cleaning supplies, broom and dust pan, and the mop and bucket with you so that you can do everything you need to do in each room before moving on. A simple formula is: desks/shelves, trash, floors, windows and then a quick check for any dust you may have missed (like baseboards, for example). Just remember, if you can see the dirt, so can they. Occasionally, sit in the desk chair and take a look around. Sometimes you will see things from their perspective that you would otherwise miss. Always check for cobwebs in corners, behind doors and ceilings. Check door facings and light switches for fingerprints.

## OFFICES

1. Remove any trash on desks, file cabinets, etc. This includes drink cans, fast food cups, anything else that may be trash.

2. Dust every horizontal surface with your duster. Look for dust build up on desks, window ledges, tops of printers and computers.

3. Clean off any fingerprints, coffee cup rings, etc. with Windex or Pledge, whatever is appropriate. Look for dirt – If you can see it, so can they.

4. Remove the trash from the trash can, replace the bag.

5. Floors - Vacuum or sweep and mop, depending on whether you have carpet or tile.

6. Your finished, move on to the next room.

BATHROOMS

1.  Put on your gloves, an absolute must!

2.  Scrub out each toilet with Comet and a toilet bowl brush, do not flush but let it sit until you are finished.  Soaking helps take out the stains.

3.  Wipe off all sinks with Clorox Clean Up and a rag.  This will be a simple, quick step unless there are stains in the sinks in which case you may need to do a little scrubbing with Comet. Rinse well.

4.  Clean the mirrors with Windex and a paper towel.

5.  Wipe off toilets with Clorox Clean Up and a rag, flushing toilets as you go.

6.  Remove trash from cans and replace bags.

7.  Sweep and mop floors.

8.  Check to see if you need to replace the toilet paper or paper towels.

9.  Your finished, move on to the next room.

# KITCHENS

1. Put on your gloves first.

2. If you have a dishwasher, make use of it. Coffee pots, any dirty dishes and coffee cups go into the dishwasher immediately. Turn it on and let it do this work.

3. Wipe off all horizontal surfaces with Clorox Clean Up including tables, countertops, chair seats, top of stove, top of microwave and coffee maker. Warning: Do not use Clorox on granite countertops, dish soap only please!

4. Clean inside the microwave with dish soap and rinse well.

5. Sweep and mop the floor.

6. Remember to come back after you have finished the other rooms to empty the dishwasher, putting away all dishes and coffee pots.

7. Your finished, move on to the next room.

# WINDOWS

1. Outside windows can be done quickly and easily using a squeegee just like those used in gas stations for car windows. (Purchase at an auto parts store for around $10.) Fill your mop bucket with 3 to 4 gallons of water and several drops of Dawn concentrated dish soap, mixing well. Scrub the windows with the sponge side and quickly squeegee them off from side to side. Once you master this technique, it can be done without streaks and is actually kind of fun.

2. Inside windows and glass doors can only be cleaned with Windex and a paper towel. Spray more than you would typically use and wipe until dry to avoid streaks. If these are windows you clean frequently, by all means then – spot clean them. Look for fingerprints and smudges, clean those and then move on. No need to spend too much time on a window you clean at least once a week.

So there you have it.  A wealth of information consolidated and simplified in terms anyone can understand.  I hope that you are encouraged to get your own business started and get ahead financially. After reading this book, the idea of owning your own business is not as complicated as you once thought.  Anyone can do this, at practically any age, as long as you have moderately good health.  If you can handle general house cleaning, you can do this and make a good living at it.  Getting out of debt and making your dreams come true takes a little effort.  But with step by step, detailed instructions, you are well on your way and over the biggest hurdle.


 I am including my e-mail address and would love to hear your success stories:


admin@guinnprofessionalcleaning.com


As an added bonus, if you have any questions please feel free to e-mail me and I will do my best to answer them.  Here's wishing you a world of success!  Good luck!

CPSIA information can be obtained
at www.ICGtesting.com
Printed in the USA
LVOW05s1550240417
531983LV00002B/55/P